The HAIDAS

People of the Northwest Coast

BY NANCY BONVILLAIN

NATIVE AMERICANS
THE MILLBROOK PRESS
BROOKFIELD, CONNECTICUT

The author would like to thank
Judith A. Brundin, Education Supervisory Specialist,
National Museum of the American Indian,
Smithsonian Institution, for her careful
reading of the manuscript and her many helpful
comments and suggestions.

Cover photograph courtesy of the Royal British Columbia Museum,
Catalog No. 16562. (Colors of original art are enhanced.)

Photographs courtesy of © The Field Museum, Chicago: pp. 8 (Neg.
No. A2734), 24 (Neg. No. A854); American Museum of Natural
History: (pp. 11 (Trans. No.'s, from top left, 1955 © Jim Coxe,
1986, 3806, both © S.S. Myers), 15 (Neg. No. 32950), 20 (Neg.
No. 46030 © Harlan I. Smith), 23 (left, Trans. No. 3859 © S.S.
Myers), 31 (Neg. No. 45326), 32 (Trans. No. K16476 © S.S. Myers),
40 (Neg. No. 324910); © Gordon Miller, Vancouver, B.C.: p. 17;
Photo Researchers: p. 23 (right, © Paolo Koch); Ulli Steltzer,
Douglas & McIntyre, Vancouver, B.C.: pp. 26, 44; British Columbia
Archives and Records Service: pp. 29, 37; David Hancock: p. 35;
National Archives of Canada: p. 46 (Neg. No. C60824); Alaska
State Library: pp. 49 (PCA 87-190), 50 (PCA 87-50); © Trevor
Bonderud/First Light, Toronto: p. 53. Map by Joe LeMonnier

Library of Congress Cataloging-in-Publication Data
Bonvillain, Nancy.
The Haidas: people of the Northwest Coast / by Nancy Bonvillain.
        p.   cm. — (Native Americans)
Summary: Presents the history and culture of the Haidas, Native
Americans who settled on the Queen Charlotte Islands off the
coast of British Columbia and in Alaska about the year 1000.
Includes bibliographical references and index.
ISBN 1-56294-491-6 (lib. bdg.)
1. Haida Indians—Juvenile literature.   I. Title.   II. Series.
E99.H2B66 1994   973'.04972—dc20   93-34902   CIP   AC

Published by The Millbrook Press
2 Old New Milford Road, Brookfield, Connecticut 06804

CONTENTS

The Haidas

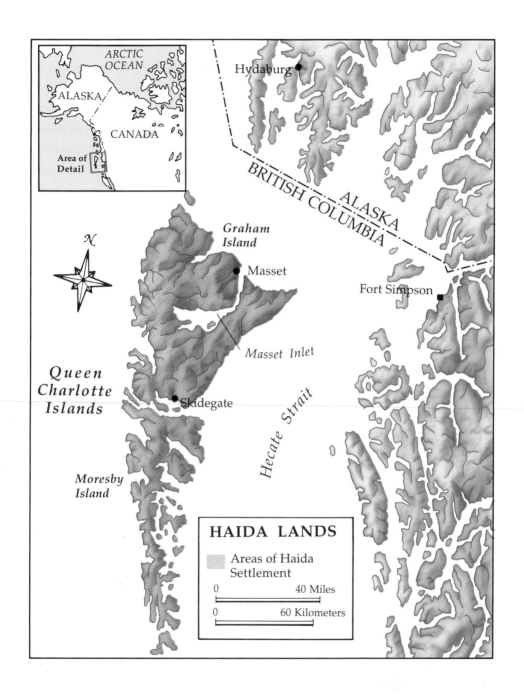

ARCTIC OCEAN

ALASKA

CANADA

Area of Detail

Hydaburg

BRITISH COLUMBIA

ALASKA

N

Graham Island

Masset

Fort Simpson

Masset Inlet

Queen Charlotte Islands

Skidegate

Hecate Strait

Moresby Island

HAIDA LANDS

Areas of Haida Settlement

0   40 Miles

0   60 Kilometers

FACTS ABOUT
THE TRADITIONAL HAIDA
WAY OF LIFE

GROUP NAME:
Haida, or Haada ("the people")

MAJOR DIVISIONS:
Eagle and Raven

GEOGRAPHICAL REGION:
The Pacific coast of British Columbia
and southern Alaska;
the Queen Charlotte Islands

HOUSE TYPE:
Large, rectangular plank houses
built of red cedar

MAIN FOODS:
deer meat, halibut, salmon, fish eggs,
shellfish, berries, fruits, nuts

*In this 1888 photo, a Haida chief poses in front of his
house with his most prized possessions — large coppers
that represent his family's wealth and history.*

Chapter One

A HAIDA FEAST

The aroma of stews and dried salmon floated through the air from the chief's house. All the villagers knew that the chief was holding a special feast. The chief was an important man among the Haida Indians. The Haidas lived on the Queen Charlotte Islands, located in the Pacific Ocean about 50 miles (80 kilometers) off the western coast of British Columbia in Canada. The Haidas often held large public feasts in order to mark family events such as births, marriages, or building a new house.

The chief's feast was a special occasion to celebrate the birth of his new daughter. He and his family sent word to their relatives and neighbors. They invited chiefs and guests from other Haida villages as well.

The guests began to arrive on the morning of the feast day. Men and women wore their best clothing—fine robes, hats made of the woven roots of spruce trees, and necklaces and earrings made of seashells and animal bone.

When the guests entered the chief's large wooden house, they saw many pots of food cooking on open hearths. The chief's wife had made stews with deer meat and wild berries collected from the woods nearby, and she had prepared dried salmon caught in the Pacific Ocean and inland rivers.

When the various dishes of meat, fish, and wild fruits were ready, the guests took their places and waited for the chief to speak. He thanked them all for making the trip to his house. The food was served, and everyone ate the delicious meal.

Then the chief said that he would like to give presents to his guests. The chief and his family distributed the gifts. They gave carved wooden boxes, bowls, spoons, and pipes; shell necklaces; baskets; and bark containers decorated with designs of animals.

Each guest received at least one present, but the more important people received many valuable gifts. The host chief saved his best gift for the highest-ranking chief among the guests. He gave this chief a large piece of shining copper, engraved with a crest that represented the host's family. These coppers were the Haidas' most valuable possessions.

As the feast day ended, the guests collected the presents they received. They were also given extra food to take home with them in bark containers. When they left, they spoke in praise of the generous host and his family.

The feast made by the chief had a special name for the Haidas. It was called a potlatch. Haida men and women hosted potlatches to express thanks for good fortune or to mark special occasions. They celebrated happy events such as births and marriages. Sad times such as deaths were also occasions for potlatches to honor the dead and comfort the families.

The chief's gifts to
his guests at a potlatch
brought him great respect
and status among his people. Shown here are a Tlingit copper
and wooden box, and a Haida carved bowl, all typical of presents valued by the northwest coast Native Americans.

Wealthy people were able to host large potlatches, sometimes with hundreds of guests. Haida chiefs sponsored especially rich feasts. In fact, potlatches could be occasions for competition among rival chiefs. Each Haida chief wanted the highest respect and status. The more a chief gave away, the greater respect he received. Therefore, wealthy chiefs gave away hundreds of blankets, bowls, carvings, and other prized objects. And they gave away the large coppers valued by all Haidas. Each copper had its own history, and the Haidas could recite the names of all the famous chiefs who had owned each piece.

HAIDA ANCESTORS ▪ The word *haada* means "the people." The ancestors of the Haadas, or Haidas, probably came to North America many thousands of years ago. They came from Asia during the Ice Age, crossing a group of islands in the Bering Strait between Alaska and eastern Russia. When the ice covering North America slowly melted away, some of the people traveled south along the coast of western Canada. They reached present-day British Columbia approximately twelve thousand years ago. Several thousand years later, the people came to the Queen Charlotte Islands. They probably arrived there nine or ten thousand years ago.

The Queen Charlottes consist of two large islands and over one hundred small ones. Most Haidas now live on the two larger islands. The Queen Charlottes are beautiful islands. Wild berries, fruits, and nuts grow everywhere. Animals such as otter, beaver, mink, and deer are found in the woods. Many varieties of fish live in the Pacific Ocean surrounding the islands. The fish also come inland, swimming upstream in rivers that go across the larger islands.

The Haidas often traveled to other places along the Pacific coast of British Columbia and Alaska. They traded goods with Indians living on the mainland. In the eighteenth century, a group of Haidas left the Queen Charlottes and built several villages in southern Alaska.

Many generations of Haidas have lived on the Queen Charlotte Islands and in Alaska. Their population grew steadily. By the beginning of the nineteenth century, approximately nine thousand Haidas resided on the islands. A smaller number, perhaps one thousand, lived in Alaska.

Over the centuries, the Haidas developed skills that enabled them to survive in their special environment. They respected the land, the sea, and the animals that they came to depend on.

But slowly the life of the Haidas began to change. Toward the end of the eighteenth century, people from Europe, Canada, and the United States started to venture into the northern Pacific Ocean near the Queen Charlotte Islands. Traders came by sea to obtain the furs of marine animals such as seals and otters. Later, other merchants came by land from the east to trade for the hides and furs of animals in the northern forests, including deer and beavers. The Haidas traded with merchants from Spain, Russia, Great Britain, Canada, and the United States. In exchange for animal skins the Haidas received manufactured goods such as iron kettles, knives, and needles.

Contact and trade between the Haidas and Europeans and Americans led to many changes in Haida society. The Haidas have now adopted many aspects of modern Canadian and American life. But the Haidas have always been determined to maintain their traditions.

Chapter Two

COMMUNITY LIFE

The Haida way of life was suited to the resources and environment of the Queen Charlotte Islands. The islands themselves are unique in geography and natural resources. On the eastern side of the islands, sandy beaches lie along the coast. On the western side, many of the islands have high mountains with sharp cliffs that slope down to the ocean.

The climate of the Queen Charlottes is mild. Temperatures rarely fall below 40 degrees Fahrenheit (4 degrees Celsius) or rise much above 80 degrees (27 degrees Celsius). It may rain in any season of the year. Because of high levels of rainfall, many different kinds of plants, bushes, and trees grow in all parts of the islands.

HAIDA VILLAGES ▪ Haida villages consisted of rows of large, rectangular houses built close to the Pacific Ocean. The houses stood along the beachfront, facing the sea. The Haidas made their houses with sturdy planks from red cedar trees. Inside a house, a large pit was dug in the center of the floor. There the Haidas built a hearth for a fire that was used for cooking,

A Haida village as it appeared in the late nineteenth century. The animals atop the totem poles in front of each house represent the families of the people who live there.

heating, and drying wet clothing. A long wooden shelf or bench was built against the inside walls of the house. The bench was used for sitting during the day and sleeping at night. Clothing, cooking utensils, and tools were stored on top of or underneath the bench.

Each house had its own name. Some of the names referred to animals or other forms of nature, such as "Dogfish House" or "Moon House." Some names referred to events in the Haidas' lives, such as "House Where One May Always Expect Food."

Outside their houses, the Haidas erected tall, thick poles made of red cedar. These totem poles stood directly in front of the house. Often as tall as 50 feet (15 meters), they were carved and painted to depict animals, birds, and fish. The creatures shown on the totem poles outside each house represented the family symbols of the people who lived in the house. The Haidas sometimes cut out a large opening in the bottom creature carved on the totem pole. The opening was a doorway for the house.

THE WORK OF DAILY LIFE ¶ The Haidas obtained their food from all of the resources in their rich environment. Men and women divided the work, and all did their share. Men caught many kinds of fish, especially halibut, salmon, cod, and her-ring. They used fishlines and hooks to catch halibut and cod in the ocean, and traps to catch salmon near the shore and in the rivers. Haidas also ate fish eggs. They used fish oil for cooking and heating.

In addition to fishing, Haida men hunted animals in the ocean and on land. Hunters caught seals, porpoises, and ot-

*Life inside a Haida house centered on the fire pit,
which was used for both cooking and heating.*

ters. In the forests of the Queen Charlotte Islands, men hunted
deer, bears, and beavers.

Both men and women gathered crabs, clams, and scallops
on beaches and in shallow water near the shore and caught
birds. There were more than twenty-five different species of
birds nesting along the coast, in forests, and on the mountain
ledges of the islands.

The Haidas also ate a large variety of plants that grew naturally in their homeland. Women had the task of gathering all plant foods. There were more than fifty different kinds of edible plants on the Queen Charlottes, including seaweed, many types of berries, wild crabapples, clover, and roots.

Salmon Patties

This is a recipe, popular among Northwest Native Americans, that uses traditional foods in a new way.

Ingredients:
  2 7-ounce cans salmon, drained and flaked
  1 tablespoon lemon juice
  1 teaspoon salt
  ½ teaspoon finely ground black pepper
  2 tablespoons grated onion
  ½ cup mashed potato
  1 egg, beaten
  1 cup dry bread crumbs
  vegetable oil for frying

Combine salmon, lemon juice, salt, pepper, onion, potato, and egg in a bowl. Blend well and chill for one hour. Form the mixture into 6 to 8 patties, each about ½-inch thick. Heat the vegetable oil in a deep saucepan to about 375°F. (190°C.). Place the patties in the oil and fry until golden brown, which will take about five minutes. Drain and serve hot.

Haida women used several different methods for cooking and storing food. The people's favorite food was halibut. The women first sliced the halibut into thin strips. Then they hung the strips on wooden racks outdoors and let the fish dry in the sun. Sometimes women preserved fish by a process called smoking. In this process, the women hung the fish in a small hut where they had first lit a fire. Smoke from the fire slowly cooked the fish over a period of several days. Salmon and cod were also prepared by either drying or smoking.

Animal meat such as deer or seal was boiled or roasted over a fire if it was eaten shortly after it was caught. If the meat was to be used later, the women preserved it by cutting the meat into strips and drying it in the sun or smoking it.

Men and women had other work to do in addition to finding or preparing food. Women made all of the people's clothing. Some clothes were made from skins of animals such as deer and seals. In order to make clothing, women first softened the skins in heated water. Then they made the skins into dresses, shirts, leggings, and robes.

Some of the Haidas' clothing was made from the roots of spruce trees and from reeds that women gathered along the Pacific coast. Women wove the roots or reeds into pieces resembling fabric. Then they sewed the pieces into capes and robes.

Haida men were responsible for building the houses. Many men worked together to construct a house. When a house was completed, the owner gave a potlatch to honor the house and thank the people who helped build it. Men also made canoes. They used timber from red cedar trees to construct the large, sturdy canoes needed for transportation on the open seas. Men who were skilled at this craft were greatly respected.

*An elaborately carved and painted canoe
typical of those built by Haida men.*

NEIGHBORS ▪ Haida men and women often traded their goods
with other Native peoples living in their region. They traveled
across the sea to the mainland of Canada to trade with
Tsimshians, Tlingits, and Kwakiutls.

The Haidas usually had friendly relations with peoples who
lived nearby. But sometimes conflicts and warfare occurred.
The Haidas carried out raids against Tsimshians and the Bella
Bella who lived on the Canadian mainland.

Raids took place for several reasons. If a person was killed
by someone from another group, the victim's relatives might

attack the murderer and the murderer's family in revenge. People sometimes planned a raid in order to acquire possessions from another group or to obtain war captives. The Haidas used these war captives as slaves in their households. The slaves had to live in their owners' houses and work for them, but they were not mistreated.

HAIDA FAMILIES ▪ The Haidas had a system of family relations based on lineages. A lineage is a group of people who are related to the same ancestor. Haida lineages came from the mother's side of the family. Children always belonged to their mother's lineage. A Haida lineage included the mother, her daughters and sons, her daughters' children, her granddaughters' children, and so on.

Members of each Haida lineage had many interests in common. They had their own name based on the place where the people believed their first ancestor lived. Family members of a lineage also owned property. In addition, lineage members could use special areas where plants, berries, and cedar trees grew or where birds nested. Also, lineages owned special dances, songs, stories, and crest figures. Most crest figures were animals, birds, or fish. But some were forms from nature, such as clouds or rainbows. The Haidas carved or painted crest figures on totem poles and on boxes, bowls, spoons, and clothing. The Haidas also used designs of their crests in body tattoos and paintings on their faces.

Each Haida lineage had one chief. When a chief died, a relative took over his position. The first in line was his oldest brother, then came younger brothers, and then the oldest son of the chief's eldest sister.

Haida lineages were linked into two large groups named Raven and Eagle. Members of the same group were not allowed to marry each other. In keeping with the Haidas' descent system, children belonged to their mother's group.

Haida communities were divided into three classes of people. The highest-ranking class, called nobles, were wealthy. They owned houses and valuable property such as crests and ceremonial blankets. Chiefs and their relatives were nobles.

The next class consisted of commoners. They did not own houses or valuables. The Haidas thought that commoners were unlucky because they lacked wealth.

The lowest class were the slaves. Slaves were people who had been captured in warfare. Children of slaves also belonged to the slave class. Slaves could not own land or houses.

HAIDA ARTS AND CRAFTS ▪ Haida artists created beautiful objects. As with other kinds of work, women and men specialized in different art forms. Men made sculptures, carvings, and paintings. Women created many kinds of baskets and woven items.

Haida sculpture and painting was decorated with formline design. Outlines of shapes were used to represent the whole body of animals, birds, fish, and people.

Perhaps the most impressive works of Haida art were the enormous totem poles containing carvings of crest figures. Carvings filled the entire height and width of a totem pole. Often this meant that the carvings were not completely realistic. For example, the head of an animal was made as wide as the shoulders. Figures carved on totem poles interlocked with one an-

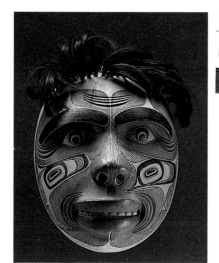

Examples of Haida art: This mask, carved to represent a human face, would be worn during ceremonies and dances. The totem pole shows how the Haidas used both animals and crest figures in their designs.

other. An animal might be shown biting the tail of another or grasping the fin of a fish.

In addition to totem poles, Haida artists carved designs and figures on bowls, spoon handles, rattles, and boxes. They also made masks of human faces. People wore the masks when participating in ceremonies and dances.

Haida women made baskets in many sizes and shapes, using roots of spruce trees and the inner bark of red cedar trees. The Haidas used baskets to carry things and to store food and personal possessions. They also made woven bags for carrying goods. Weavers made blankets and capes from yellow cedar bark. These blankets were used within the household and for trade with other groups.

A Haida woman weaving a red cedar basket. She rotates the basket on the pole as she works, using the stone to keep the basket balanced.

Haida women also made fine hats of woven spruce roots. The hats had high tops and flared brims, and were sometimes decorated with paintings. Women made hats for their families' own use as well as for trade with other Native peoples.

■ ■ ■

The Haidas valued all of their traditions, from the activities of hunting, fishing, and gathering wild plants to their close relations with those they depended on in times of need. Generous and helpful to friends and neighbors, they valued respect and kindness above all else.

A Haida Game

This game is adapted from a popular Haida game of the nineteenth century. It was probably played with a strip of leather, but you can use wide elastic.

Materials:
one piece of elastic,
    approximately 3 inches (7.5 centimeters) wide and at
    least 3 feet (1 meter) long
two sticks to hold the elastic
one thin stick with a knob at one end
    (the knob can be made by wrapping tape around
    the end of the stick)

The two sticks are hammered into the ground at a distance apart that is a little greater than the length of the piece of elastic. The piece of elastic is stretched between the sticks and attached to them.

The players form two teams, each group sitting on opposite sides of the elastic, 3 feet from it. They take turns throwing the knobbed stick at the elastic target. The object of the game is to hit the elastic. If the stick misses completely, or hits the elastic and jumps back less than half the distance between the target and the player, the player gets no points. Another player then has a turn. If the stick hits the target and jumps back more than halfway, or if the player catches the stick as it jumps back, it counts four points, and the player gets another turn.

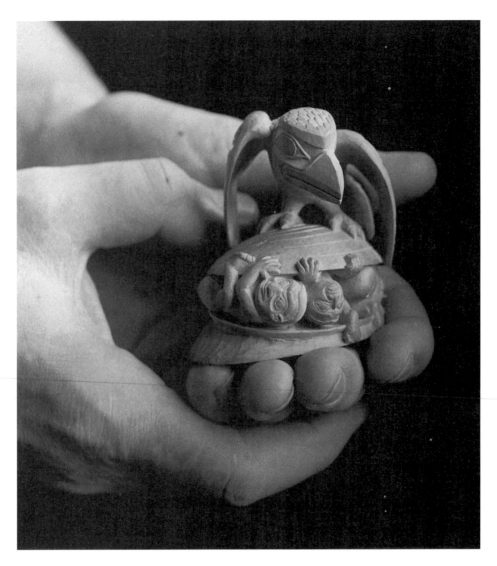

This boxwood carving by well-known Haida artist Bill Reid is called "Raven Discovering Mankind in the Clam Shell" and is meant to depict the creation of the Haida people.

Chapter Three

THE SPIRITUAL WORLD
OF THE HAIDAS

The Haidas' religion taught them to respect all creatures of the earth, seas, and sky. It taught them to respect spirit beings who protected the world. The Haidas' religious ceremonies honored the spirits and thanked the people in their communities.

THE HAIDA UNIVERSE ▪ The Haidas believed that the universe was divided into three parts. The earth occupied the middle area. It was flat and circular in shape. The islands and mainland that made up the world of the Haidas was here. Another part existed above the earth. This area was solid, and was supported by a pillar extending up from the earth. The third part, below the earth, was seawater.

The Haidas believed that they were protected by many different kinds of spirit beings. Some spirits were linked to living creatures, such as the bear, raven, and owl. Other spirits were found in places such as mountains, lakes, or caves.

People prayed to spirits for aid and protection. When the Haidas prayed, they made offerings of tobacco and birds' feathers in order to please the powerful spirit beings. Spirits responded to prayers and offerings by giving help, advice, and comfort.

CEREMONIES ▪ The Haidas performed many different kinds of ceremonies. Some were carried out to honor the spirits. Others were connected to events in people's lives. Ceremonies were held at birth, at the age of puberty, at marriage, and at death. These rituals consisted of feasts, dances, and activities specific to each event.

BIRTH. The Haidas believed in reincarnation. To them, a new baby was a replacement for a relative who had died. People knew who the baby represented by some physical resemblance or some personality trait similar to that of the dead relative. The Haidas' beliefs showed the importance they placed on ties between relatives. These ties did not end with death. They continued afterward through a connection between a newborn baby and an ancestor.

When a woman was about to give birth, one of her husband's female relatives came to help her. After the birth, the infant was given its name at a small feast held by the family. The Haidas rejoiced in the birth of babies, especially if they were girls. But all children were gladly welcomed.

Soon after birth, a small ceremony was held when the infant had its ears pierced. Daughters and sons of high-ranking, wealthy people were also tattooed on their arms and legs.

CHILDHOOD. Young children spent much of their time at play. Girls and boys were taught special songs and dances by their

Babies were welcomed with great joy into Haida families. This 1793 print shows a Haida chief named Hatria with his wife and infant daughter. Their cheeks are painted red, and the woman is wearing an ornament in her lower lip.

elders. As they grew up, they learned the tasks and responsibilities they would have when they became adults.

Boys belonging to important lineages went to live with one of their mother's brothers in order to learn skills and gain knowledge of family ceremonies and legends. Boys also learned how to endure physical hardships. From time to time they would stop eating in order to build up their ability to withstand hunger. They practiced swimming in the cold winter sea so that they would be able to survive in harsh conditions.

PUBERTY. When a young girl began menstruation, about the age of twelve, an important, month-long ceremony was held for her. She was taken to a special part of her house, which was separated from the rest of the living area by a painted screen. There she remained for one month, during which time only her female relatives could visit her. Her mother, grandmother, sisters, and aunts came to see her and to offer advice and instruction. It was the duty of her mother and her father's sisters to teach her about womanhood.

During her seclusion, a Haida girl had to follow certain rules to toughen her for the difficulties of adult life. She slept on a pillow of stone, and she was not permitted to laugh or even to talk except in emergencies.

When the month had passed, the girl took a ritual bath. Then her family held a potlatch to express their happiness and respect for their daughter.

MARRIAGE. According to Haida custom, parents arranged marriages for their sons and daughters. In some cases, a mother's brother might arrange a marriage for his niece or nephew. The Haidas believed that a young man or woman should always follow the advice of older relatives.

A Haida marriage ceremony consisted of a public feast hosted by the bride's family. At the feast, relatives of the bride and relatives of the groom gave valuable gifts to each other. The exchange of gifts honored the two families.

DEATH AND FUNERAL RITES. The Haidas showed respect for the dead as well as for the living. Funerals were the most elaborate of Haida rituals. When an individual died, women belonging to the dead person's father's lineage came and prepared the body for the funeral. First, they washed and dressed the body. Then they painted the dead person's face with crest designs of his or

A carving to honor the dead. Here the deceased is guarded by the figures on each end of the coffin and watched over by the raven crest figure.

her lineage. Afterward, the body was placed in a coffin in a rear section of the house. Relatives and neighbors came to express their grief. They cried loudly and spoke of their sorrow.

Later, men took the coffin out through an exit in the rear of the house. They placed the coffin in a grave house situated behind the main house. The grave house belonged to the lineage. It contained the remains of members of the group.

Afterward, the dead person's family held a public funeral potlatch. When a man died, his heir hosted the potlatch. When a woman died, her funeral potlatch was hosted by her husband. At the feast, personal property belonging to the dead person was given to lineage relatives. A woman's property was given to her daughters. A man's property went to his brothers and his sister's sons.

A Haida headdress worn during ceremonial dances.

The Haidas believed that when the funeral ceremony and potlatch were over, the person's soul departed from the village and journeyed by canoe to the Land of Souls.

If the dead person had been an important man or woman in their lineage, a totem pole was carved and erected in front of their house. This pole contained crest figures belonging to the dead person's lineage.

DANCES ▪ People performed several kinds of dances and songs at many Haida ceremonies. Dance performances were long and complex. Major dances were given at potlatches when a new house was built and after a funeral.

Some dances were connected to the Haidas' belief that spirits could invade or possess a human being. At the beginning of such dances, the Haidas believed that a spirit associated with the dancer's lineage possessed the dancer's body. The dancer would shake in fear and then disappear from view through an exit in the house. Later, the dancer would return, still shaking and possessed by the spirit. A man who specialized in ritual treatments would soon arrive and try to make the spirit leave the dancer's body. After several attempts, the healer would claim success in getting rid of the spirit, and the dancer would return to his normal state. He would perform a dance of rejoicing, and give gifts to people in thanks for their concern.

▪ ▪ ▪

The Haidas' religious beliefs and ceremonies taught the people many lessons about their world. They learned their proper roles in life. They learned to show respect to spirits and to ancestors. And through their ceremonies they honored all the creatures of the universe.

Chapter Four

AN EXPANDING WORLD

Toward the end of the eighteenth century, the Haidas first met travelers from European countries. In 1774, a Spanish seaman named Juan Perez sailed into the waters of the north Pacific Ocean. Perez stopped at Langara Island, one of the Queen Charlotte Islands. Traders and explorers from other European nations soon followed Perez. They came from Russia, Great Britain, and France. Others came from eastern Canada and the United States.

TRADING WITH EUROPEANS ▪ The Europeans who came to the Pacific Northwest wanted to obtain furs from animals in the northern region. They especially sought sea otter furs, which they sold for handsome profits in European cities and in the Far East. But they needed the help of the Haidas and other Native peoples to acquire furs. The Natives caught the animals and traded the skins to Europeans.

Both men and women took part in trade with Europeans in the 1800s. Haida men caught the otters, and the women pre-

*Native Americans of the Pacific Northwest hunted sea otters
for their fur, which was much valued by the Europeans.*

pared the skins for market. Both men and women met with Europeans and bargained over the terms of trade. The Haidas wanted a variety of European products. They prized goods made of copper or iron, including knives, kettles, needles, and other tools and utensils. The Haidas also liked to use copper for earrings, ornaments on clothing, and decorations on bowls, pipes, and spoons.

By 1798, the Haidas knew how to make iron, and thus were able to make their own iron products. After that time, they no longer depended on Europeans as their source of metal goods. But the Haidas continued to obtain firearms, cloth, and blankets from the Europeans. Blankets were especially valued. Indeed, half of all the trade goods received by the Haidas were blankets.

In addition to household and personal items, the Haidas and Europeans exchanged a variety of foods. In the early years, the European traders did not have their own sources of food and needed the Indians' help in order to survive. The Haidas traded dried and smoked fish and meat to Europeans. The Haidas also began to grow potatoes in gardens in their villages. By 1825, they were supplying a large quantity of potatoes to European merchants and sailors.

The trade in sea otter furs continued into the early years of the nineteenth century. But after 1810, the number of sea otters greatly declined because of overtrapping. By 1830, the sea otter trade had ended. However, Europeans still wanted animal furs. Now they traded for furs of land animals such as beaver, deer, and mink.

The Haidas were not the only Native peoples in the region who traded with Europeans. Nearly all neighboring groups also

Fort Simpson as it appeared in 1863.

exchanged their own products for European goods. In the early years of trade, the Europeans usually remained on their ships and met the Indians at sea. Since the Haidas lived on the Queen Charlotte Islands and were excellent seafaring people, they had an advantage in this form of trade. In fact, for a time, the Haidas acted as "middlemen" between the Europeans and Natives living on the Canadian mainland. But in the last years of the eighteenth century, the Europeans built trading posts on the mainland coast and in the interior. The first to do so were the Russians, who operated posts in Alaska, which was then a territory owned by Russia. Soon afterward, the British opened posts in British Columbia.

Once trading shifted to the mainland, the Haidas lost their advantage. Then they had to trade through Native peoples who lived in the territory where the European posts were located. The Haidas dealt with the Europeans through the Tsimshians, a group with whom they had traded long before the Europeans had arrived in North America. On occasion, though, the Haidas' relations with the Tsimshians turned sour. Raiding and warfare between the two peoples sometimes occurred.

The Haidas soon established their own trade relations with the Europeans at posts on the mainland. The first important post was Fort Simpson. It was built in 1834 by merchants from the Hudson's Bay Company, a large trading company operating throughout Canada. By 1835, the Haidas supplied merchants at Fort Simpson with potatoes, dried fish, and meat. The Haidas also traded potatoes to merchants of the Russian-American Company and to Russian military forts in Alaska.

CHANGES IN HAIDA CULTURE ▪ Contact between Haidas and Europeans gradually led to changes in Haida society. Important changes occurred in the Haidas' way of life. Soon after the fur trade began, the Haidas shifted much of their time and energy to hunting and trapping the animals that they could trade to European merchants.

Other changes also occurred in Haida communities. The people who were most active in trading with Europeans were able to greatly increase their wealth. With greater wealth, chiefs and nobles hosted rich potlatches and gave away many valuable gifts to their guests. And since they were able to be so generous, the importance of wealthy Haidas also rose.

Changes also took place in Haida artwork. After artists obtained woodworking tools made of iron, they created larger totem poles. Wealthy Haidas hired artists to build tall totem poles to place in front of their houses and to honor important people in their lineage who had died.

In the early nineteenth century, Haida artists began to carve objects for sale to European traders, sailors, and settlers. They produced small versions of totem poles and various kinds of carved items such as boxes, platters, pipes, bowls, and spoons. Artists made their products from traditional materials such as wood, but they also carved objects out of argillite, a black stone found in the region.

By the middle of the nineteenth century, Haida women were weaving ceremonial robes from the woolen blankets that they had received in trade from European merchants. The Haidas especially favored thick red robes. Women decorated

A Haida boy poses with ceremonial robes woven from woolen blankets received from the Europeans.

the robes with copper and silver buttons. In addition, they sewed metal buttons into designs on other kinds of clothing, such as dresses and tunics.

Changes in the Haidas' economy, social system, and artwork were adopted into Haida culture and became part of their new way of life. Although these changes were responses to European contact, they added to the traditions of the Haidas.

But another result of European contact was disastrous to the Haidas. The Europeans introduced several deadly diseases into Haida communities. The worst of these were smallpox, measles, and influenza. The diseases did not exist in North America before Europeans arrived. Many Europeans who came to North America were carriers of the deadly germs. Since the Haidas and other Native Americans had never had these diseases, they did not have any natural resistance. When the diseases were introduced into their villages, the people quickly became sick. Thousands of people died. In many cases, whole families and even whole villages were destroyed.

Chapter Five

ADJUSTING TO CHANGE

Many changes took place in Haida communities in the late 1800s. The trade in animal furs with Europeans and Canadians declined, but the Haidas still wanted European products. So they grew more potatoes to sell at the posts and forts. And Haida artists produced more crafts to sell to traders and sailors.

Canadian and American settlers began to invade territory held by the Haidas and other Native peoples in western Canada and Alaska. They built many towns in the region. Haidas visited these towns to sell their products and to obtain manufactured goods. By 1860, they were trading at Victoria on Vancouver Island, off the coast of British Columbia, and at Sitka in Alaska. In 1869, merchants from the Hudson's Bay Company opened a post in the Haida community of Masset in the Queen Charlotte Islands.

THE HAIDAS IN BRITISH COLUMBIA ▪ As more settlers invaded the western regions, they took land that belonged to the Haidas and other Native peoples. When the Haidas protested to government authorities, officials sided with the settlers. By the late 1800s, the Haidas were outnumbered by settlers. The Haidas lost much of their original hunting territory.

Additional changes took place in Haida life when Protestant missionaries from Great Britain and Canada established churches in Haida communities. They wanted to convert the Haidas to Christianity.

At first, the missionaries had little impact on the Haidas' religious beliefs. Most of the people continued to follow their ancient beliefs and conduct their traditional ceremonies. But by the late 1800s, missionaries had set up schools in Haida villages. Some of these were boarding schools, and the children lived in them during the school year. The missionaries hoped that if they separated Haida children from their parents, they would convince the children to give up their traditions and beliefs. Gradually, many Haidas did adopt Christianity. However, they also kept their Native ways of living.

In the second half of the nineteenth century, new outbreaks of disease spread through Haida communities. The deadliest of these was a smallpox epidemic in 1862 and 1863. It began in the Canadian town of Victoria on Vancouver Island and quickly spread to the Haidas living on the Queen Charlotte Islands.

Several additional bouts of smallpox, measles, and flu occurred in the 1870s and 1880s. Many Haidas died from these diseases. By 1890, their population was only 1,200, down from nearly 9,000 in the 1840s. Modern scientists believe that most of the deaths resulted from the deadly smallpox epidemic of 1862–1863.

Shortly afterward, the government of British Columbia established reserves for Native peoples living in the province. The term "reserve" comes from the words in the treaties between the Indians and the government. In the treaties, the Indians agreed to give up most of their land, but they "reserve for themselves" a portion of their original territory. In 1876, the Joint Commission for the Settlement of Indian Reserves in the Province of British Columbia was established to meet with Native peoples to decide the terms of treaties and reserves.

This 1890 photograph shows a Haida medicine man (on the right) with his new friends, the Christian missionaries.

The Commission also set up two separate bands of Haidas. A band is a group of Native people who live in the same area. It has one government, and the people in the band act together for the common good. Each Haida band takes its name from the largest village in the community. One band was called Masset, and the other was named Skidegate.

VILLAGE AND FAMILY LIFE. Changes also took place in the Haidas' village and household life. By the 1890s, most people were living in small houses with one family. By the twentieth century, lineage relatives no longer lived together in the same house.

Many of these changes in houses and family life came as a result of pressure from Canadian officials, teachers, and missionaries. These authorities wanted the Haidas to give up their own ways and adopt a Canadian style of living. And changes occurred in some of the Haidas' ceremonies. In 1884, the Canadian government, convinced by Christian missionaries that the Haidas were indulging in strange religious practices, outlawed potlatches and Haida dances. Despite the new law, many families continued to hold private feasts in their homes to celebrate births and weddings and to mourn the deaths of family members.

By the late 1800s, many changes had taken place in the kinds of work the Haidas did. Now most households had small gardens where women planted crops for their family's use. They also kept farm animals such as cows and horses.

The work of Haida men also changed. They no longer hunted and trapped animals in the woods. Instead, many men took jobs in the towns and cities of British Columbia. The largest number of Haidas were employed in the fishing industry. Some worked on fishing boats for Canadian companies. Others owned their own boats but sold their catch to the Canadian companies. Both men and women worked in fish canneries (factories that canned fish) in the early twentieth century. And some Haida men worked for mining companies and sawmills in British Columbia.

THE HAIDAS IN ALASKA ▪ The Haidas living in Alaska also experienced many changes in their way of life in the late nineteenth century and early years of the twentieth. In 1867, Alaska was sold by Russia to the United States for $7,200,000. Then, in 1880, gold was discovered near the Alaskan town of Juneau, and many American prospectors and settlers rushed into the area. Before that time, only 400 settlers lived in all of Alaska. Just ten years later, the 1890 census reported that 4,200 Americans and 1,800 people of mixed American and Native ancestry resided in Alaska.

As thousands of settlers invaded land owned by Haidas and other Native peoples, the Indians lost much of their own territory. The government in Alaska did not protect the Indians' rights. When the Natives lost their land, they had to seek work from American mining, logging, and fishing companies in order to earn money to purchase food and other goods. The most important sources of work for Haida men and women were the salmon canneries that opened in Alaska in 1878.

▪ ▪ ▪

A Haida woman canning salmon in a factory in Alaska in the early twentieth century.

By the beginning of the twentieth century, the Haidas in British Columbia and Alaska had lived through many changes. The governments of Canada and the United States had taken away most of their land and changed their lives through rules and laws. But despite these problems, the Haidas found new ways of living and strived to improve their situation.

In this 1897 photograph of the Haida village of Howkan,
Alaska, the beginnings of change can be seen. Totem poles
still stand in front of the houses and canoes still line the
beaches, but now the houses have glass-paned windows.

Chapter Six

THE HAIDAS TODAY

During the twentieth century, the Haidas in British Columbia and Alaska have adopted many aspects of Canadian and American lifestyles, but they have also kept some of their valued traditions.

The Haida population has steadily increased from its lowest point, recorded in 1915. In that year there were only 588 Haidas in British Columbia. By 1992, approximately 3,000 Haidas lived in the two bands of Masset and Skidegate, and about 350 Haidas were reported in Alaska.

The Masset Band consists of twenty-six villages and fishing sites. The Massets own a total of 2,214 acres (896 hectares) of land. The Skidegate Band includes eleven villages and fishing sites, with a total of 1,677 acres (679 hectares) of land. Although the two bands are separate, they joined together in 1980 to form the Council of the Haida Nation.

Each Haida village contains a school, community hall, and church. Some Haidas operate small businesses such as stores, restaurants, and gas stations.

Most residents work outside the reserves. People from Masset travel to the Canadian mainland for as much as six months a year to work in canneries and the fishing industry. Many residents of Skidegate work for nearby timber and logging companies.

In recent years, both the fishing and logging industries have declined in the region. The number of jobs available to the Haidas has decreased. As a result, many Haidas have left the reserves to find jobs in other places. By 1992, more than half of the Haidas were living away from the Queen Charlottes.

But the Haidas continue to identify themselves as members of their home villages and lineages. The people follow their traditional principle of family relations through women. And most Haidas still speak their native language.

Even though the Haidas have adopted many aspects of Canadian life, they also keep some of their own traditions. Haida artists have continued the crafts of carving and painting. They have produced new totem poles, canoes, and decorated boxes and platters. Several Haida artists have great reputations throughout Canada and the United States, among them Robert Davidson and Bill Reid. Their work is widely praised and sought by museums and individual collectors.

The Haidas in British Columbia again perform some of their traditional ceremonies and dances. Women make ceremonial button blankets and decorated robes. Children learn the ancient stories and songs of their people. And men and women are again hosting potlatches and funeral feasts.

■ ■ ■

In 1912 the Haidas and other Native peoples in Alaska joined together to form an organization called the Alaska Native

A ten-year-old boy performs a greeting dance during a 1993 reenactment of a Haida Meeting of the Nations ceremony in Vancouver.

Brotherhood. It was the first Indian organization in the United States. The Alaska Native Sisterhood was founded in 1923. Both groups were formed to improve living conditions among Native peoples. They also wanted to protect the Indians' rights to their own land.

In the 1940s, Haidas asked the United States government to recognize their land rights, saying that they were the first owners of 900,000 acres (364,230 hectares) of land. In 1949, the U.S. government set boundaries for a Haida reservation of 101,000 acres (40,875 hectares). However, three years later a United States federal court denied the Haidas rights to a reservation because they said the Haidas were not a separate group.

The Alaska Native Brotherhood immediately protested on behalf of the Haidas and the nearby Tlingit Indians. They stated that the Haidas and Tlingits had rights to 20 million acres (8 million hectares) of land in the Tongass National Forest and the Glacier Bay National Monument. The Brotherhood said that the United States had wrongfully taken land from the Haidas and Tlingits to set up these two national parks.

It took many years, but the land claims case was finally settled in 1966. The court ruled that the United States government had acted illegally by taking the land of the Haidas and Tlingits. The court also stated that the American government had neglected its duty to protect Native peoples from American settlers and miners.

A commissioner was appointed to determine the value of land taken from the Haidas and Tlingits. The Natives said that the land was worth $80 million. The government claimed it was worth only $3 million. After reviewing the case, the commissioner decided the land's value was $16 million. However, the court ignored the commissioner's opinion, and awarded the Haidas and Tlingits only $7.5 million. This figure amounted to only 43 cents per acre. Although the Haidas and Tlingits objected to the small sum, they decided to accept the award. They used most of the money for educational and health programs in their communities.

In the 1960s, American oil and gas companies asked the United States government for permission to drill for fuels in Alaska. But first the government needed to determine the boundaries of Native lands.

In response to these developments, Indians in Alaska formed the Alaska Federation of Natives in 1966. They wanted to protect Native rights to land in the state. They met with government officials and legislators to discuss the matter. All participants finally agreed to a settlement in 1971. The agreement was approved by Congress as the Alaska Native Claims Settlement Act. Under the act, twelve regional groups of Native members were set up. Each group controls a special territory and can determine the use of its land. Each also receives money from the oil and gas companies for fuels found in its region.

The community of Hydaburg (a town established by the Haidas in 1936, with its own constitution and tribal council) joined the Tlingits in forming the Sealaska Regional Corporation. Sealaska has 16,000 Native members, most of whom are Tlingits. Together they have 280,000 acres (113,316 hectares) of timberland in addition to their villages. Some 60,000 of these acres (24,282 hectares) are located just north of Hydaburg. Another regional corporation, known as the Haida Corporation, owns 23,000 acres (9,308 hectares) south of Hydaburg. The Haida Corporation has 560 Haida members. As a group, they own several companies including Haida Oil, Haida Seafoods, and the Haida Corporation Timber Division. Profits from these ventures are used to fund social, educational, and health programs in Haida communities.

Despite these recent changes, though, most residents of Hydaburg still rely on many of their traditional economic activities: fishing for salmon and halibut, catching crabs and shrimp, hunting deer, and gathering wild berries and fruits.

The Haidas in Alaska have also kept some of their Native rules and ceremonies. They follow rules of lineage relations through women. The people host potlatches and participate in ceremonial dances. Most Haidas over fifty years of age speak the Native language, although many younger people do not. In 1980, the Haidas formed the Sealaska Heritage Foundation to teach and promote Native skills, arts, and crafts.

■ ■ ■

The Haidas of British Columbia and Alaska know the value of their traditions. They have adjusted to many changes in their lives resulting from contact with Europeans, Canadians, and Americans. Now the Haidas look forward to the future, aware that they have kept their communities strong.

A HAIDA STORY:
THE SONG OF THE BEARS

Long ago there was a young man and woman who loved each other very much. She was the daughter of a chief. The man was the son of a commoner. Although they loved each other, they knew that they could not get married because they both belonged to the Raven crest.

The parents of the two young people reminded them that it was time for each of them to marry someone else. But they did not want to marry if they could not marry each other. The parents confined them to their own houses, but the couple managed to slip away and meet in the woods. They built a hut for themselves and stayed there.

When winter came, the young man decided to visit his family in the village. The girl did not want to face her angry parents so she remained in the forest. The boy promised to return before nightfall of the fourth day.

When he returned to his village, his parents again locked him in the house. After many weeks, he was able to escape to the woods to search for his sweetheart. But when he returned to their hut, she was nowhere to be found. The young man was horrified. He looked in the nearby woods and by the streams but could not find her.

After searching for days, he returned to his family's village and asked his people to help him find the girl. His father joined him, disturbed because he had confined his son to the house.

Again the search proved useless.

But even after many years had passed, the man mourned for his lost love. One day, he went to a great medicine man to ask for help. The medicine man asked for a piece of clothing that had been worn by the young woman. He held the garment in his hand and said:

> I see a young woman sleeping on the ground. It is your love. There is something in the bushes, coming toward her. It is a bear. The bear takes hold of her. She tries to get away but cannot. The bear takes her with him, a long way off. I see a lake. They reach it and stop at a large cedar tree. She lives in the tree with the bear.

The man went to the cedar tree near the lake described by the medicine man. He called to his love to come down. Finally, she descended and returned to her village. Then she told of her years with the bear. She said that at first she was heartsick to be parted from her family, but when the bear saw how sad she was, he did all in his power to cheer her up. As the years passed, she began to feel at home in the tree house. The bear tried to make her comfortable and please her. He composed a song, which to this day is sung by Haida children. It is the "Song of the Bears." It has these words:

> I have married a young Haida woman. I hope her relatives won't come and carry her away from me. I will be kind to her. I will give her berries from the hill and roots from the ground. I will do all I can to please her. For her I made this song, and for her I sing it.

This is the "Song of the Bears." Whoever sings it has the bears' lasting friendship.

IMPORTANT
DATES

c. 1000 Haida ancestors settle on the Queen Charlotte Islands

c. 1750 A group of Haidas leaves the Queen Charlotte Islands and migrates to southern Alaska

1791 First smallpox epidemic strikes Haida communities

1834 Hudson's Bay Company builds Fort Simpson

1867 United States purchases the territory of Alaska from Russia

1869 Hudson's Bay Company opens a trading post in the Haida village of Masset on the Queen Charlotte Islands

1871 Canadian Parliament passes the Indian Act, defining the relationship between Native peoples and the Canadian government

1882 Meeting between Haidas and members of the Joint Commission for the Settlement of Indian Reserves in the Province of British Columbia. Haidas agree to boundaries of 37 reserves, containing a total of 3,484.5 acres (1,410 hectares) of land

1884 Canadian Parliament outlaws potlatches and ceremonial dances

1936 Haidas form the town of Hydaburg, Alaska, and adopt a constitution and tribal council

1952 Haidas of Hydaburg join with Tlingits to file a land claim against the United States for 900,000 acres (364,230 hectares) of land

1966 U.S. Court of Indian Land Claims rules in favor of Haidas and Tlingits in the land claims case

1971 U.S. Congress passes the Alaska Native Claims Settlement Act; Haidas of Hydaburg join the Sealaska Corporation and the Haida Corporation

GLOSSARY

Band: a term used in Canada to define a group of Indians who live together and are governed by a council of elected leaders.

Commoner: one of the classes of people among the Haidas. Commoners do not own houses or valuable property.

Coppers: large disks made of copper, with engravings of animals, birds, or fish to represent the owner's lineage.

Crest figure: an animal, bird, or fish that represents a Haida lineage. Crest figures are carved or painted on houses, totem poles, boxes, platters, and other personal property.

Descent system: a system of kinship that defines links between people to a common ancestor.

Lineage: a group of people who are descended from a common ancestor.

Missionary: a member of a religious sect who attempts to convert Native peoples to the missionary's faith.

Noble: the highest of Haida classes of people. Nobles own houses and valuable property. They are wealthy and highly respected by others.

Potlatch: a ceremonial feast hosted by an individual or family to mark special occasions. The potlatch host gives valuable presents to guests.

Reincarnation: the belief that a deceased ancestor is reborn into a new baby.

Reserve (Reservation): an area of land owned by a group of Native people. The term "reserve" is used in Canada; the term "reservation" is used in the United States.

BIBLIOGRAPHY

*Books for children

*Batdorf, Carol. *Gifts of the Season: Life Among the Northwest Indians.* Blaine, Wash.: Hancock House, 1990.

*_____. *Totem Poles: An Ancient Art.* Blaine, Wash.: Hancock House, 1990.

*Beck, Mary L. *Heroes & Heroines in Tlingit-Haida Legend.* Bothell, Wash.: Alaska Northwest Books, 1989.

Blackman, Margaret. *During My Time: Florence Edenshaw Davidson.* Seattle: University of Washington Press, 1985.

*McKeown, Martha F. *Come to Our Salmon Feast.* Portland, Ore.: Binford & Mort, 1959.

Murdock, George. *Rank and Potlatch Among the Haida.* New Haven: Yale University Press, 1936.

*Shetterly, Susan H. *Raven's Light: A Myth From the People of the North-west Coast.* New York: Macmillan, 1991.

Stearns, Mary Lee. *Haida Culture in Custody: The Masset Band.* Seattle: University of Washington Press, 1981.

*Stewart, Hillary. *Indian Art of the North West Coast.* Vancouver: Douglas & McIntyre, 1985.

*_____. *Looking at Totem Poles.* Vancouver: Douglas & McIntyre, 1993.

Suttles, W., ed. *Handbook of North American Indians.* Vol. 7. Washington, D.C.: Smithsonian Institution, 1990.

Swanton, John. *Contributions to the Ethnology of the Haida.* New York: American Museum of Natural History, Memoir 8, 1909.

INDEX